CREATIVE PROB SOLVING.

A useful little strategy book by **craig+bridget**

INTRO

DUCTION.

Strategy is a big, serious word, but the principles behind the practice are surprisingly simple. We have distilled 25 years of working in strategy to 25 lessons for doing it well. We hope it's a bit like your favourite restaurant giving you all their recipes. You can try a few of them at home, but you still enjoy eating out, and perhaps appreciate the effort that went into it a little more than before.

GET
EXPLORI

STAY CURIOUS.

The world is your raw material.
Everything around you can tell a story.
If you're constantly wondering how this
got there or why they did that, you might be
gathering material for your next strategy.
If this way of thinking doesn't come naturally,
you might be in the wrong job.

CHANCE FAVOURS THE PREPARED MIND.

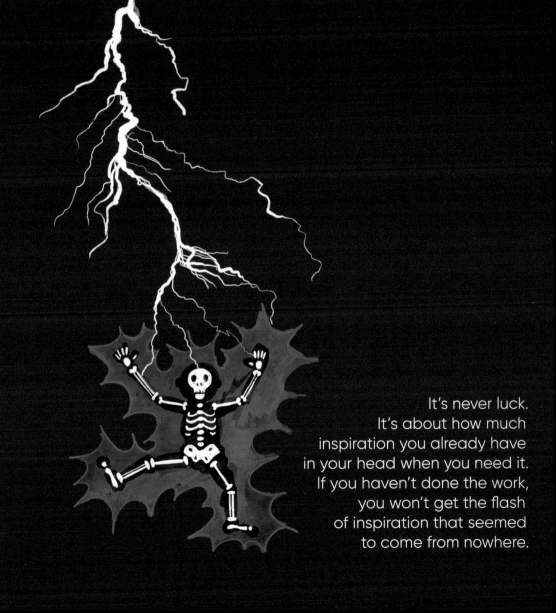

It's never luck.
It's about how much
inspiration you already have
in your head when you need it.
If you haven't done the work,
you won't get the flash
of inspiration that seemed
to come from nowhere.

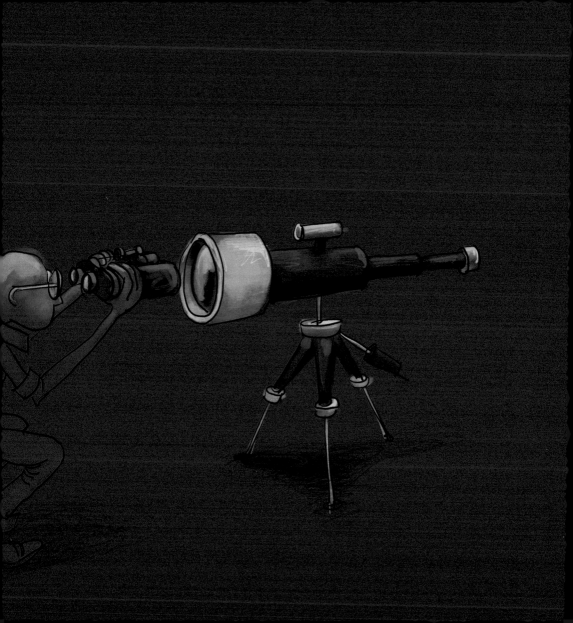

GET OUTSIDE OF YOUR HEAD.

Look at the problem from someone else's perspective.
Ditch your baggage and your personal point of view.
This is much easier to say than do.

CREATE
OPTIONS.

A good strategy makes
the world open up before you.
Things that seemed tricky
suddenly seem possible.
Good strategy creates more options.
Bad strategy reduces your options.

BE INTERE

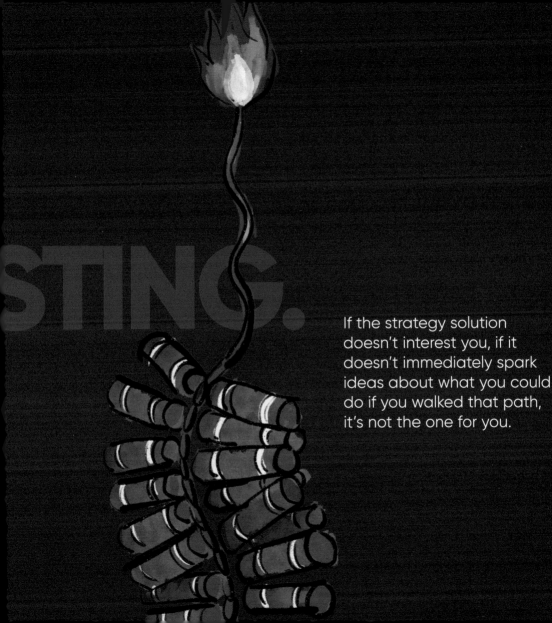

If the strategy solution doesn't interest you, if it doesn't immediately spark ideas about what you could do if you walked that path, it's not the one for you.

DIG DEEPER.

USE
THE
DATA.

You need to know as much as you can.
Drink it all in. Immerse yourself.
Then create. Leap. Be lateral.
For creative strategy,
data is the context,
not the content.

FORGET
THE
DATA.

DO THE MATH.

Creative strategy doesn't mean
making it up as you go along.
To be creative, you need to know
what you're working with.
Playing with the numbers
can help with that.

WORK OUT WHERE YOU WIN.

You will have advantages.
No matter how tricky the challenge seems.
You will win somewhere.
Start there.

BE
REALISTIC.

Creative strategy is about
using what you have to get more.
It's not about magically becoming
another organisation entirely.
Start with your real limitations
and resources.

THE FRUITS

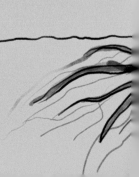

ARE IN THE ROOTS.

The secret to most brands' success
lies somewhere in their past.
You just need to find it and
make it relevant again.

BURN SOME BOATS.

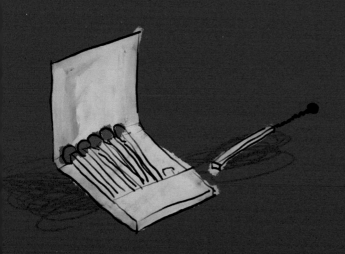

When military commanders arrived in hostile
territory, it was tempting to retreat. To give up.
So they ordered their soldiers to burn the boats.
When there's no going back, you get more ingenious.
Which boat should you burn?

TELL A

STORY

Strategy is a story.
If it's a good one, people
remember it and act on it.
If it's a stodgy pile of charts
and data, it sits on the shelf.
Good stories change the world.

BE BRAVE.

What is the most audacious path to follow?
How can you be more ambitious?
You and your brand are probably capable
of far more than you have done so far.

IMAGINE YOU'RE WRONG.

I know, right?
Hard to believe.
We normally spend our time
looking for confirmation.
But if you hunt for contradiction,
you grow faster.

FOCUS ON WHAT WON'T CHANGE.

We have Jeff Bezos to thank for this. He was right.
Whilst your competitors get distracted by
the short term, focus on what endures.
Then you win in the long term.

BRING IT

TO LIFE.

OUT LOUD.

Conversation forces cognition.
As you explain your plan,
you create your plan.
Ideally say it to someone who knows
little of your organisation and challenges.
Does it make sense to them?

CREATE HOPE & EXCITEMEN

Creative strategies are descriptions of a possible future. To motivate people to act, it helps if that future is bright, and the path to get there well defined.

BUILD YOUR VOCABULARY

More than anything else,
words are your currency.
Words are ideas.
The more you know,
the more ideas you have
at your disposal.
The right words change the world.

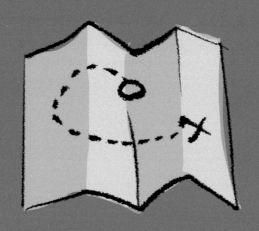

USE A DIAGRAM.

The say a picture tells a thousand words. A four box grid or a Venn diagram might well save a lot of words. Yes, it's always an over-simplification. But so is a map. And maps often help you get to your destination faster and more directly.

INVITE EVERYONE IN

WE

None of us are as good as all of us.
And if you work in an organisation,
things will move faster if everyone gets
involved in making the strategy.
Command and control is
very old fashioned.
And it doesn't work.

TAKE THE PRESSU OFF

AMUSE

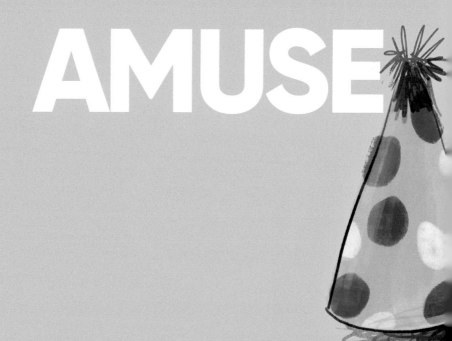

YOURSELF.

If it's not fun, then you're probably not doing it right. You're the first audience for your ideas. If they don't excite and amuse you, then...

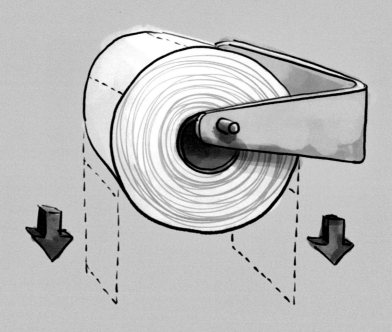

THERE IS NO RIGHT ANSWER.

That's liberating, isn't it?
Creative strategy is about generating
interesting options. It's not an equation that
can be solved. It's a creative discipline, so
many different answers can be the right ones.
If you believe. If you commit.

CHASE IDEAS NOT STATUS.

It really shouldn't be about proving you're the smartest person in the room. Lose that impulse and chase down the best ideas instead.

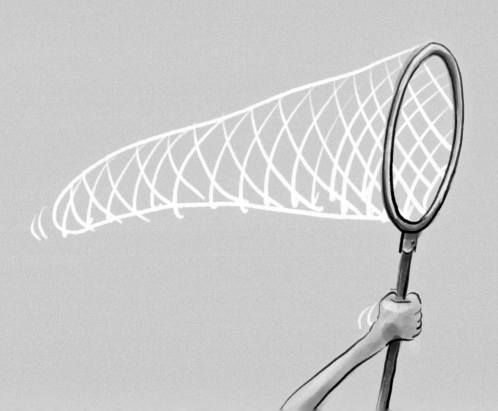

The future doesn't exist.
It is the sum total of all
the decisions we make.
Nothing is destined.
Instead, it gets made
by creative strategy.

THE FUTURE CAN BE MADE.

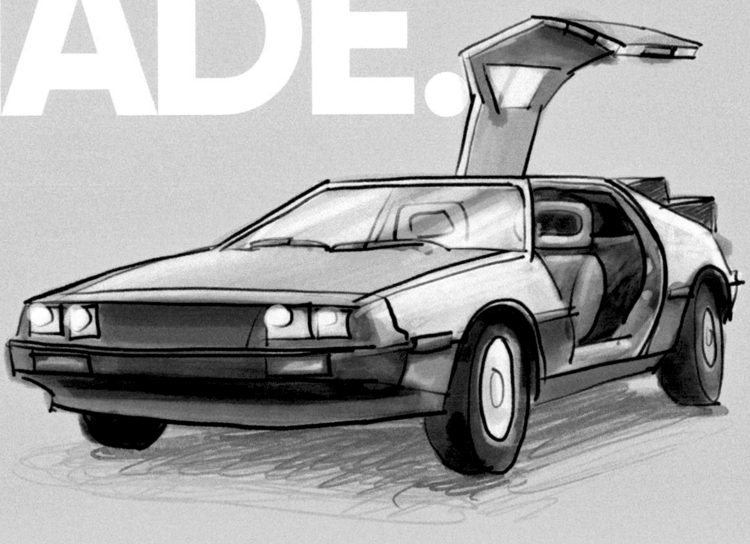

CHOOSE GOOD PARTNERS.

An outside perspective is always useful.
Teamed with your inside knowledge
it can get you to new places.

We can help with that.